Elizabeth Cady Stanton
A Biography for Young Children

This book is dedicated to
those educators and parents
committed to continuing the work
so ably begun by our heroine,
Elizabeth Cady Stanton.

Published by Gryphon House, Inc., 3706 Otis Street,
Mt. Rainier, Maryland 20712

Library of Congress Catalog Number: 91-71104

Design: Graves Fowler Associates

Publisher's Cataloging in Publication
(Prepared by Quality Books Inc.)

Schlank, Carol Hilgartner.
    Elizabeth Cady Stanton : a biography for young children / by Carol
Hilgartner Schlank and Barbara Metzger. --
    p. cm.
    SUMMARY: A biography of one of the first leaders in the women's
rights movement.
    ISBN 0-87659-151-9 (pbk.)
    ISBN 0-87659-152-7 (library binding)

    1. Stanton, Elizabeth Cady, 1815-1902--Juvenile literature. 2.
Feminists--United States--Biography--Juvenile literature. 3.
[Stanton, Elizabeth Cady, 1815-1902.] 4. [Feminists.] I.
Metzger, Barbara. II. Title.

HQ1413.S67   305.420924
                             QBI91-546

Elizabeth Cady Stanton

A Biography for Young Children

By Carol Hilgartner Schlank
and Barbara Metzger

Illustrated by Janice Bond

gryphon house
Mt. Rainier, Maryland

Long ago when women and little girls wore long dresses, Elizabeth Cady Stanton was born. Her mother and father were happy she was a healthy baby, but they were sorry to have another girl.

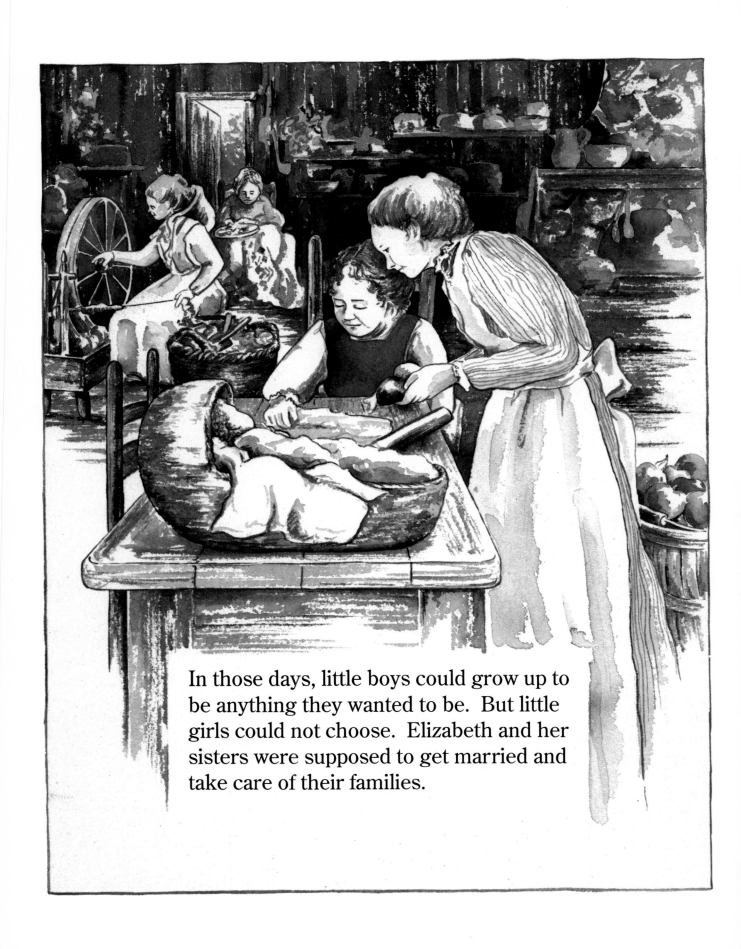

In those days, little boys could grow up to be anything they wanted to be. But little girls could not choose. Elizabeth and her sisters were supposed to get married and take care of their families.

Elizabeth was a lively little girl. In the summer time, she and her younger sisters played in the woods and at the pond near their house.

On rainy days, they loved to dress up
in the old clothes in the attic.

In the winter time, the girls made snow
people and climbed on snow mountains.
On special days, Elizabeth would get to
ride in a horse-drawn sleigh.

Sometimes she went downtown to the court house where her father worked.

She liked to visit the jail
and to go into the shops
and the hotel.

Because Elizabeth would rather climb trees than practice being a lady, her mother and her nannies often got cross with her.

When Elizabeth fussed about mending her stockings or helping in the kitchen, her mother would say, "Go to your father. Perhaps he can make you behave."

But often Elizabeth's father was too busy
to scold her. He would tell her to sit
quietly and read books. Elizabeth would
settle down happily. Reading was one of
her favorite things to do!

One terrible day, Elizabeth's big brother, Eleazar, died. Her parents were brokenhearted. Eleazar was their pride and joy.

Elizabeth's father had planned for Eleazar to work in his office with him. Elizabeth put her arms around her father and tried to make him feel better. Her father looked at her sadly. "Oh, my daughter," he said. "You should have been a boy."

That day Elizabeth decided she would be as much like her brother as she could be.

She studied hard at school and won a
prize for her good work.

She beat the boys at games and learned
to ride her father's fastest horses.

Elizabeth's father was proud of her. But when she was old enough to go to college, he wouldn't let her go because she was a girl.

Elizabeth was angry and disappointed, but she continued to read books and learn new things.

When Elizabeth grew up, she got
married. Her family grew until she had
seven rambunctious children to care for.
They were a real handful.

But somehow she found time to work
hard to change the way people treated
girls and women. Elizabeth knew she
could not change peoples' ideas all by her-
self. So she got other women to help her.

While Elizabeth was at home caring for her family, she wrote letters and speeches.

Her best friend, Susan B. Anthony, traveled around the country talking to people about their ideas.

Later when Elizabeth's children were grown up, she and Susan went on these trips together.

Because Elizabeth Cady Stanton worked so hard for so long, women and girls today have many more choices.

If she were alive today, Elizabeth would be happy to see women voting, owning property, and working as doctors or lawyers, builders or astronauts, mail carriers or police officers.

And if she were alive today, she would still be working for women's rights.